Praise for Airea D. Matthews and *Bread and Circus*

"The reigning Poet Laureate of Philadelphia packs heart and humor into this collection of autobiographical poems while taking a scalpel to the idea of a benevolent free market."

—*Philadelphia Magazine*

"This discerning and significant collection presents a tender resistance to commodification by straight lines ('Indecisive. Afraid'), controlled images ('copious selfies'), and colonial stories ('tidy myths')."

—*Poetry Foundation*

"In this formally inventive book, Matthews deploys a surprising mix of lyrics, prose poems, images, and docupoetic forms to consider the self as a product shaped by individual experience and systemic forces. Adam Smith's 1776 *The Wealth of Nations* provides a frame for the collection, which blends autobiography with economic and social theory to examine the origins and far-reaching effects of capitalism and its intersections with race, gender, and class. Smith's texts appear throughout the book, altered by Matthews to reveal a disturbing subtext about the commodification of human life."

—*Poets & Writers*

"Through 'extraction's and 'extraction and extension's of Guy Debord's *The Society of the Spectacle* and Adam Smith's *The Wealth of Nations* as well as contrapuntal and prose poems, [*Bread and Circus*] interrogates childhood and parenthood, fear and hope, and language and mythology. I read this slowly, and I read each poem at least twice, and still it, along with its accompanying black-and-white images, is one I want to revisit."

—*Book Riot*

"A vigorous and personal refutation of late-stage capitalism . . . Full of humane wisdom, this powerful volume forces readers to acknowledge systemic inequity."

—*Publishers Weekly* (starred review)

"In her stunning collection *Bread and Circus*, Airea Matthews uses a bricolage of citations and erasure to reflect on the epigenetic costs of Black dispossession in a country founded on self-interest. *Bread and Circus* is an authentic journey of enduring love and witness. It is sonorous, erudite, raw—and one that will stay with me always."

—Cathy Park Hong, author of *Minor Feelings*

"When sinking into the work of Airea Matthews within *Bread and Circus*, *gratitude* is the word that most eagerly leaps to mind. I am grateful to be witness to a writer dismantling the boundaries of form, shape, and language, while not sacrificing any brilliance on the page. This is a stunning collection of work, which feels both ahead of its time and also abundantly on time."

—Hanif Abdurraqib, author of *A Little Devil in America*

"From page to unrelenting page in this fierce and brilliant book, Airea Matthews shows us just how high the stakes of poetry should be. If you are not writing to save your life, you are not writing in Airea Matthews's league. That simple. Her vision is encompassing: What are the systems that subordinate us to their own perpetuation? Her vision is intimate: Where, then, are our opportunities for grace? If these beautiful poems are to be believed, that grace is to be found, or rather forged, against all odds, at every turning. That is the scale of the achievement here."

—Linda Gregerson, author of *Canopy*

"Like all crowning collections in an oeuvre, this book enacts, with tenderness and intelligence, an erudition that matches the capacious love of its ambitions. Formally ambidextrous, toothed with wit and uncompromising dignity, Matthews engages the archive as a breathing document, refusing to let history be done with itself, and thereby accomplishes what I love most about poetry—especially hers: that it lives, is living."

—Ocean Vuong, author of *Time Is a Mother*

"The Roman poet Juvenal criticized a public distracted with free wheat and mindless entertainment. Toni Morrison said the point of racism is to keep us distracted from fully living our lives. With the genius and ferocity of mother love, Airea Matthews's *Bread and Circus* shreds our expectations of what poems can be and do, while clearing the air of the illusions that cloud our understanding of past, present, self, and other. Lift the cover and breathe in the clarity concentrated on these pages."

—Gregory Pardlo, author of *Digest*

"Below these immensely humane, dramatically compelling, and formally adventurous poems (one turns the page eager to discover which unexpected route Matthews has taken into her subject next) lies not just a hard-won practical wisdom but something rarely, if ever, seen in contemporary poetry: an astonishing and clear-sighted economic literacy. All of which leaves *Bread and Circus* not just a riveting book about family and individuation, self-interest and altruism, commodity and community, but—at a time when our understanding of their larger context is becoming crucial to our survival—one of critical importance."

—Don Paterson, author of *The Poem*

"I have never read a book of poems that was this honestly, brilliantly, beautifully intimate. These poems of family, friendship, history, and bond (in all that word's layered and clamoring manifestations) show us that getting inside the deepest rooms of our histories takes courage and a fierce kind of loyalty. There is no limit to what Airea D. Matthews can do. *Bread and Circus* is the truth of it."

—Gabrielle Calvocoressi, author of *Rocket Fantastic*

Also by Airea D. Matthews

Simulacra

BREAD
AND CIRCUS

Airea D. Matthews

SCRIBNER
New York   London   Toronto   Sydney   New Delhi

Scribner
An Imprint of Simon & Schuster, LLC
1230 Avenue of the Americas
New York, NY 10020

First Scribner trade paperback edition May 2024

SCRIBNER and design are trademarks of Simon & Schuster, LLC.

Simon & Schuster: Celebrating 100 Years of Publishing in 2024

For information about special discounts for bulk purchases,
please contact Simon & Schuster Special Sales at 1-866-506-1949
or business@simonandschuster.com.

The Simon & Schuster Speakers Bureau can bring authors
to your live event. For more information, or to book an event,
contact the Simon & Schuster Speakers Bureau at
1-866-248-3049 or visit our website at www.speakers.com.

Interior design by Kathryn A. Kenney-Peterson

Manufactured in the United States of America

1   3   5   7   9   10   8   6   4   2

Library of Congress Cataloging-in-Publication Data has been applied for.

ISBN 978-1-6680-1145-4
ISBN 978-1-6680-1146-1 (pbk)
ISBN 978-1-6680-1147-8 (ebook)

For Fred. Forgiven.

and every thing, now bridles its desires, and limits its anxious longings to two things only—bread, and the games of the circus!

—Juvenal

Contents

PSALM

BREAD
AND CIRCUS

Legacy Costs

P

And then
there are those
who in the words of
a r t i s t
Mendel-Black, "inherit
r e b e l l i o n ."
Large lots of unbeing
p a s s e d
one generation to the next.
Absent value on the free
m a r k e t
nothing gets resolved.
Too many other worries
a n y h o w :
the who what when
w h e r e
of basic living. Elegant
names are expensive.
It costs too
much to be pronounced. yet
Nobler
to forbear the weight
of obscurity, put on the
f u l l
armor of mundane
Gods who war against
their heirs wasting
a w a y
brothers
among from lamb.
fattened

Q

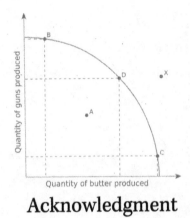

Acknowledgment

It is not from the benevolence of the butcher,
the brewer, or the baker, that we expect
our dinner, but from their regard to their own interest.

—Adam Smith

March, 1969

back at the church the best man draped the groom's shoulders. passed a flask of hundred proof. a mother fondled her fake pearls. walked the aisles in search of a soloist to replace the cousin who canceled an hour earlier. *will you sing His Eyes on the Sparrow or Amazin' Grace,* she asked each guest.

across town on Hanover Street,

a young woman in a taffeta and lace gown huddled on the cold tile of a YWCA bathroom stall. she heard the lobby phone ring incessantly. the receptionist trumpeted her name over the intercom. she balled up wads of Angel Soft and blotted the Revlon fleeing her lash. for the last two hours, the cost of the dress, flowers, drinks, the soloist, the hall, and her mother's second mortgage to fund the matrimonial circus paraded across an embedded reel. thoughts of a fatherless baby pushed her to decision.

that inevitable bride called a yellow taxi to deliver her to fate. outside, a homeless prophet touched her shoulder while she waited, reassured: *it's better for the baby girl, Honey.*

three hours later, an understudy organist played the sorriest wedding march. the bride tripped down the aisle. busted her knee wide open. bled through her stockings and silk slip. her groom, many swigs in, balanced by his best men, could barely stand. her mother ran to the altar to lift her daughter, her sole investment. while an unholy congregation craned their necks and swished their church fans, advertising a local funeral home, to watch a lovely commodity reluctantly agree to her own barter.

Debord's Redacted Spectacle

The image of bliss ful social unification through consumption merely [suspends] the consumer's awareness of the actual divisons until his next disillusionment with some particular commodity. Each new product is ceremoniously acclaimed as a unique creation offering a dramatic shortcut to the promised land of total consummation. But as with the fashionable adoption of seemingly aristocratic first names which end up being given to virtually all individuals of the same age, the objects that promise uniqueness can be offered up for mass consumption only if they have been mass-produced. The prestigiousness of mediocre objects of this kind is solely due to the fact that they have been placed, however briefly, at the center of social life and hailed as a revelation of the unfathomable purposes of production. But the object that was prestigious in the spectacle becomes [the] mundane [once the object] is taken home by its consumer — at the same time as by all its other consumers. Too late, it reveals its essential poverty, a poverty that inevitably reflects the poverty of its production. Meanwhile, some other object is already replacing it as justification of the system and demanding its own moment of acclaim.

The Troubles

Man watches his history on the screen with apathy and an occasional passing flicker of horror or indignation.
  —Conor Cruise O'Brien, Irish historian

It's January 1972 and inside
Ma's television buzzes. Oddly
accented men wearing crucifixes
call for work and housing. Children's
coattails drag along the seats
of burnt-out cars walling in
their free Derry. Tanks thrum
through the rubble thrown, stones
ricochet off umbrella shields, bullets
plunge into some husbands' flesh like
rose thorns burrowing chest deep.
A priest waves a handkerchief
as flag of surrender, begging
passage for the shallow-breathed
whose blood slicks his boot.
Unknowns will die cradled
in the arms of strangers
who moments earlier sang
We shall overcome, someday,
faithfully clinging to the same
distant hope that finds Ma
thousands of miles away
on a different continent,
wailing on her bedroom floor,
arms flailed across her belly,
mourning an unwanted
who spine-swims against her
backbone's curve,
holding vigil for blood
that will not come and
me who surely will.

Severance

200 years after Franklin signed
the Declaration of Independence
Amtrak purchased the crumbling stone
viaducts and decrepit bridges between
Boston and Washington. In five years
the federal government would surface
245 miles of track, lay 171,000 ties,
renew 2,868 joints, interlock
5,800 switch timbers and order 492
Amfleet cars including sixteen sleek
Metroliners like one of the two
housed at Trenton Rail Station
where the authorities found
my father in stuporous nod
while on the official clock.
Having decided several offers
of rehab enough, Amtrak severed
all contractual encumbrances.

It was 1977 when my father stumbled
from the station into a recession but
first into Pete Lorenzo's bar
to pilfer time through a bottle
then plot provision—
three square, four souls—
strategizing who to feed
to whom.

Smith on Exchange

Man some-

times uses the same arts with

his brethren, and when he has no other means of

engaging them to act according to his inclinations, endeavours by

every servile and fawning attention to obtain their good will. He has

not time, however, to do this upon every occasion. In civilised society

he **stands at all times in need of the** co-operation and assistance of

great multitudes, while his whole life is **scarce sufficient** to gain the

friendship of a few persons. In almost every other race of animals,

each individual, when it is grown up to maturity, is entirely indepen-

dent, **and** in its natural state has occasion for the assistance of no

other living creature. But man **has almost constant occasion for the**

help of his brethren, and it is in **vain** for him to expect it from their

benevolence[:] only. He will be more likely to prevail if he can interest

their self-love in his favour, and shew them that it is for their own

advantage to do for him what he requires of them. Whoever offers to

another a bargain of any kind, proposes to do this. **Give me**

that which I want,

and you shall have

this which you want is the meaning of every such offer; and it is in

this manner that we obtain from one another the far greater part of

those good offices which we stand in need of.

Swindle

Learn the suits, Ace:
a club looks like a three-leaf clover
a spade is an upside-down heart
a diamond looks like two kissing triangles
a heart is a goddamn heart.
A hand is five cards:
one card, each finger.
The Ace is the highest
followed by head cards—
King, Queen, Jack—then
count back by 10.
That's the rank.

You get what I'm givin'?

Bring a Barbie doll
something to play with.
Circle the players from afar.
Eye your sneaky Uncle Nate
nigga tucks cards under his cuff.
Pull on his sleeve, ask for a hug
if it feels stiff say you're thirsty.
Don't crawl under that table
'less you want a gun in my mouth.
Don't sniff the powder on the felt.
And, boy, don't touch those chips;
they worth more than us both.

You see what I'm sayin'?

Aim for loose play
every motherfucker's hungry.
When the game is tight
stakes get too fat, too quick.

You'll lose before the draw.
Spy those hands, Ace. Tell me
what you see. Scratch your chin
rub your nose, pull on your ear—
we got a code.

Eat.

Thing is that Ace is tricky
hinges on what's held;
it can play high or low.
A full house ain't shit.
Bend the straight.
Fuck a pair.
Fear that flush.
If you see those head cards
in order with the same suit
grab your baby doll
go to the bathroom
flush the toilet twice
stick one finger down
your throat
bloat your cheek, run out
force lunch on the table. Say:

Daddy, my head hurts.

We make dust, baby boy.
Only lose what little you left.

Ain't No Snitch, 1978

We are sitting in one living room of our two-family house.
The Edge of Night, my grandfather's favorite soap,
has just ended and he lifts himself off his La-Z-Boy to head
to the bedroom. I hear the closet open, a shoebag unzip,

the smell of Old Spice fresh from the red bottle wafts
down the corridor. It's summer and my tiny legs are
sticking to my grandmother's shrink-wrapped couch when
Pop-Pop says *Dee Dee let's take a ride to see Ms. Durum.*

She lived across town, across the Trenton Makes Bridge.
Everyday our routine the same. I'd walk downstairs to Pop-
Pop and Mom-Mom's apartment. Eat a scrambled egg,
some juice, and watch *Sesame Street* until his stories

came on. Then, we'd drive to see Ms. Durum or
Ms. Rye. I'd always liked Ms. Durum more.
Her treats were sweeter. She'd have a glass dish
filled with Now and Laters on her kitchen table.

Sometimes her teenaged son, Bran, was home.
When Pop-Pop and Ms. Durum would go upstairs to
"look at somethin' needs fixin,'" Bran would babysit.
We'd perch on that velour couch and binge *Mister*

Rogers, or Bran would read comics aloud since I feigned
illiteracy and shyness. For fun, Bran might kiss my neck
or put one finger down my panties. He was cute. I liked
his tickling. Ms. Durum would be moaning, making

some kind of noise upstairs. Once, I heard wood bang
against the wall in a pattern—bump, breath, bump,
breath. It sounded like a song. Bran wasn't there that day,
so I just listened and devoured candy while Mister

Rogers slid his hand under Henrietta Pussycat's dress.
Pop-Pop joked that "nahenlatas" bought my silence. I
promised to hush long as his mistresses gave good sugar.
He smiled, knowingly, pinched my cheek.

On Origin and Use

When the division of labour has been once thoroughly established, it is but a very small part of a man's wants which the produce of his own labour can supply. He supplies the far greater part of them by exchanging that surplus part of the produce of his own labour, which is over and above his own consumption, for such parts of the produce of other men's labour as he has occasion for. **Every man** thus lives by exchanging, or becomes in some measure a merchant, and the society itself **grows to be** what is properly a   commercial   society.

But when the division of labour first began to take place, this power of exchanging must frequently have been very much clogged and embarrassed in its operations. One man, we shall suppose, has more of **a certain commodity** than he himself has occasion for. while another has less. The former consequently would be glad to dispose of, and **the latter** to purchase, a part of this superfluity. But if this latter should chance to have nothing that **the former** stands in need of, no exchange can be made between them.

The butcher has more **meat** in his shop than he himself can consume, and   the   **brewer** and **the baker** would each of them be willing to purchase a part of it. But they have nothing to offer in exchange, except the different productions of their respective trades, and **the butcher** is already provided with all **t h e   b r e a d** and beer which he has immediate   occasion for. ...

the number of **cattle** which had been given in exchange for them. **The armour** of Diomede, says Homer, cost **o**nly nine **ox**en; but that of Glaucus co**s**t a hundred oxen. **Salt** is said to be the common instrument of commerce and exchanges in Abyssinia; a species of shells in some parts of the coast of India; dried co**d** at Newfoundland; tobacco in Virginia; **sugar** in some of **o**ur **[water]** India colonies; hides **o**r dressed **leather** in some other countries; and there is at this day a village in Scotland, where it is not uncommon, I am told, for a workman t**o** carry **nail**s instead of money to the baker's sh**o**p or **ale**-house. ...

The man who wanted to buy salt, for example, an d had nothing but cattle to give in exchange for i t ,

must have been obliged to buy salt to the value of a whole ox, **o**r a whole **sheep** at a time. He could seldom buy less than this, because what he was to give for it could seldom be divided without loss.

The Family Room in '79

Before there was a room, there was a family. That family had a mother. That mother's children called her Mama. Some nights, Mama cowered in the corner of the family room. Her head rested on the faux-wood-paneled organ sitting unplayed against the east wall. The sheet music for *The Nutcracker*, yellowing on its shelf. To the left, the bookshelf housed dust interrupted by tiny hand-prints, *Encyclopædia Britannica*, and one knockoff copy of *Gray's Anatomy* dog-eared to da Vinci's sketch of the *Vitruvian Man* with the next page high-lighting the number of bones in the body. In the crook of the window framed by chipped lead and the diseased gums of a rotting house, Malibu Barbie tanned in the moonlight posed at an awkward 30-degree angle, all but forgotten. No matter if the window was open or closed, the room always smelled fetid like something was going bad slowly, out of sight.

In the changing late autumn Mama found new ways to reimagine the fresh corn she'd been gifted from various aid societies—soups, stews, hidden with other vegetables. Although we all knew Papa despised the vestiges of a hand-out, we couldn't predict when and if he would make his way back home. But we all knew he hated one specific symbol of his failure—corn.

One November Sunday, Mama made roasted pork loin, buttered rice, and suc-cotash. Just as she was setting the food on the table, we heard Papa's heavy sideways gait on the stairs. Mama set another place. Papa peered into the kitchen and before he could sit down, before he saw the fork gleam, he barked, "Woman, get to the room." Mama quick shuffled. Sister and I heard them ar-guing in the family room while we picked the lima beans, one by one, from the succotash at the kitchen table. You needed only to separate the beaded divider and peek around the door frame of the kitchen to see every other room in the house. Walls so thin it was like there weren't walls at all. We heard him bay about a man not being able to come home and enjoy his meal. Mama, em-boldened, spoke her mind that night. Told him he hardly comes home anyway. Sister said she heard Mama ask about another woman with a pretty-sounding name, asked him what he ate over at her house. Then we heard four monstrous thuds against the wall as if a large animal had been hurled a distance.

As quickly as he came, Papa jetted down the stairs. An agonizing screech registered from the back of the house. Sister and I looked across the table at one another, lips trembling to hold back tears. We ran to the family room to find Mama hunched in a corner, slurring the command "Call the ambulance!" which came out sounding like "Shawltampants!" Her voice favored the pub men during afternoon crawl when Papa would sit us atop the bar, order Shirley Temples, and smile as we learned our ABC's from the toothless bartender. We inched closer to Mama to make sure we understood her. Again, garbled: "Call the ambulance!" That's when we noticed Mama's wishbone arm slung like a contortionist, tucked between her two knees. Her hand was cupped like a basin, collecting the plum rivering from her lip. Sister and I looked away, too afraid a long gaze would make her feel like a sideshow attraction, or like the trapped raccoon that had come to die in our backyard that summer. We averted our eyes, fixed our pity toward the window. Asked her, "What happened?" She mumbled "Corn." Sister and I nodded and agreed, "He don't eat corn."

Sister rose first to fetch the emergency numbers in the kitchen drawer that swung clumsily from two rusted nails. She picked up the phone and dialed 3 numbers. Mama's yaw was lowering. She was on the verge of "the hurt sleep," as Sister and I called it. Desperate to rescue something, I grabbed Malibu Barbie from the windowsill, tucked *Gray's Anatomy* under my arm, and walked into the bedroom we shared with Mama.

I'd been working on teaching myself subtraction by carving lines in the bedpost while *Good Times* played on the small black and white TV. I could already count to the number 206 from the anatomy book, the number of bones. I had etched ten lines. Using the webbed plastic hands of that tanned doll, I carved a new line. Eleven now. I turned the television up full blast, climbed atop the mussed bedspread, pulled my legs to my chest—fetal—sucked my thumb while rocking and whispering, "It'll be okay. That was only the 11th. Mama still got a lot of bone left."

Say When

I don't exactly know when
we crossed the boundary.
When need became pleasure.
But Mama's plump quieted
that house. Made caterwauls
retreat to the holed ceiling
of the hallway closet where
the attic bats roosted.

Brown vespers emerged
when my family lay as one;
Daddy submerged in fire
water, that's what he called it
when asked. When his hands
trembled. When the chirping
above our drowsing heads did
not signal dreaming but peril.

When the gleam of an abandoned
screen replayed an episode
of Kiss parading in makeup.
When I nightmared the spectacle
of Gene Simmons's tongue
convexing his chin. When Ace's
guitar caught aflame. When jinn
rocked opera as berceuse.

When a child craves to be
safely nuzzled, crook of arm.
When scent of sweat is sweeter
than heifer's milk, I would curl
my seven-year-old body under
warm flesh, suckle my mama's
breast—that gentle tug, our
singular sick comfort.

On Supper

Nobody ever saw one animal by its gestures and natural cries signify to another, this is mine, that yours; I am willing to give this for that. **When an animal** wants to obtain something either of a man or of another animal, it has no other means of persuasion but to gain the favour of those whose service it requires. A puppy fawns upon its dam, and a spaniel **fawns upon its dam** by a thousand attractions to engage the attention of its master who is at dinner, when **it wants to be fed.**

Man sometimes uses the same arts with his brethren, and when he has no other means of engaging them to act according to his inclinations, endeavours by every servile and fawning attention to obtain their good will. He has not time, however, to do this upon every occasion. In civilized society he stands at all times in need of the cooperation and assistance of great multitudes, while his whole life is scarce sufficient to gain the friendship of a few persons. In almost every other race of animals each individual, **when** it is grown up to maturity, is intirely independent, and in its natural state has occasion for the assistance of no other living creature. But man has almost constant occasion for the help of his brethren, and it is in vain for him to expect it from their benevolence only. He will be more likely to prevail if he can interest their self-love in his favour, and shew them that it is for their own advantage to do for him what he requires of them. Whoever offers to another a bargain of any kind, proposes to do this. Give me that which I want, and you shall have this which you want, is the meaning of every such offer; and it is in this manner that we obtain from one another the far greater part of those good offices which we stand in need of. It is not from the benevolence of the butcher, the brewer, or the baker that we expect our dinner, but from their regard to their own interest. We address ourselves, not to their humanity but to t**he**ir self-love, and never talk to them of our own necessities but of their advantages. Nobody but a beggar chuses to depend chiefly upon the benevolence of his fellow-citizens. Even a beggar does not depend upon it entirely. The charity of well-disposed people, i**n**d**eed**, s**u**pplies him with the whole fund of his subsistence. But though this principle ultimately provides him with all the necessaries of life which he has occasion for, it neither does nor can provide him with them as he has occasion for them. The greater part of **his occasional wants** are supplied in the same manner as those of other people

18

Ars Poetica, 1979

Digging in dregs of trash
to find the bird my father needed
to get well, I tore a vanishing
line across the length of my palm.
My hand emerged slowly,
crown of pulp, pulsing. My ex-
communicated ex-Navy father:
Come here, Boy (though I was a girl
he called me boy because
he wanted one). He pressed
his dirtied fingernail against
the head of the valley, dispensing
some trauma he'd picked up
in Vietnam about dead bodies
not being able to feel and pain
being the only true way to know

aliveness. How pleasure persuades
belief in a Heaven that doesn't
exist and that he could prove
God was fiction and Satan
the realest motherfucka ever
made: *Look around.* He lifted
his index, the one staunching
the flow, to his lip. Tasted my iron.
I let out something—more
moan than wail—too shaken
for much else when he grabbed
the back of my neck, pulled me
close to teach his only lesson
worth remembering: *Cry, Boy,*
look that honest wound in the eye
and you betta let this mutilated
world see what she did to you.

Papa Teaches the Hard Six at a Gulf Station, 1980

That lady under the bus shelter
runs through johns for dimes
      hair wild. dried specks on her chin.
      front teeth missing. drugs.

Those two boys fake pumping gas
plan to rob that woman in the Seville
      asked directions. local accents.
      plates were out-of-state. expired.

The man with the cup and sunglasses
can see better than you or me
      pen in his left pocket. same color
      as the sign he's holding. inked fingers.

The mother in that Corolla got twins
with different fathers, coddles the one
      through her rearview. other's
      belt trapped in the door.

The church pastor on Parkside
just liquored down his deacon
      no wedding rings. empty bottles
      behind the seat. trojans underneath.

Boy, to reap high, size up the hard six
risk hustle with three pair of eyes:
      the pair that sees listens to the pair
      that hears heeds the pair that warns.

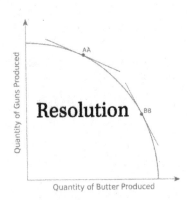

...the desire of bettering our condition ... comes with us from the womb and never leaves us until we go into the grave.

—Adam Smith

On Division

This **division** of labour, from which so many advantages are derived, is not originally the effect of any human wisdom, which foresees and intends that general opulence to which it **gives occasion**. It is the necessary, though very slow and gradual consequence of a certain propensity **in human nature** which has in view no such extensive utility; the propensity **to** truck, **barter, and exchange one** thing **for another.**

Whether **this propensity** be one of those original principles in human nature, of which no further account can be given; or whether, as seems more probable, it be the necessary consequence of the faculties of reason and speech, it belongs not to our present subject to enquire. It **is common to all men, and to be found in no other race of animals** [.]

which seem to know neither this nor any other species of contracts. Two **greyhounds**, in running **down t**he same hare, have sometimes the appearance of **act**ing **in** some sort of **concert**. Each turns her [the hare being hunted] towards his companion, **or endeavour**s **to** intercept her when his companion turns her towards himself. This, however, is not the effect of any contract, but of the accidental concurrence of their passions in the same object at that particular time. Nobody ever saw a dog make a fair and deliberate **exchange** of **one** bone **for another with another** dog. Nobody ever saw one animal by its gestures and natural cries signify to another, this is mine, that yours; I am willing to give this for that. When an animal wants to obtain something either of a man or of another animal, it has no other means of persuasion but to gain the favour of those whose service it requires.

Working-Class Bedtime Story, 1981

every morning, two hours after
  the gate closed on her night
shift, a gowned woman wiped
    oil from ladder rungs, sharpened
     two hatchets with a dull whetstone
& steadily climbed through
  troposphere to reach the far edge
   of her roof. positioned just so—
     legs in kenebowe, arms dual
     wielding—she'd cut the sun
     from its cosmic string, watch
   it gyrate in midair. light
don't down nowhere easy.
  taking swing after swing
   until the ax head flew &
  sun dimmed & fell
through that roof
  onto a parlor floor
   where that woman
collapsed, sheerly
done in. while
  her curious young 'un
   with a feral stare
    sat silent in the dark
   corner chair,
  picking flint-flakes
of ash from her
nappy-ass hair.

Camelot

Summer of '82
he came back
to my mother's mother's
house, missing a finger.

He and my grandmother
drank Old Crow for hours,
swiveled in the torn white
vinyl seats in her kitchen,
forearms draping the edge
of her glass-topped table.

I'd asked what happened,
eyeing the empty near his pinkie.
He said *sleepin' on the tracks*
a transit train ran over this hand.
He was able to pull back—mostly—
all except for the ring finger,
which sat under a rail in Metuchen.

My grandmother inched in, offered:
So what, Sonny, you holdin'
whiskey like a man ain't
lost a damn thing.
He laughed like royalty
at court, head thrown back.
Turned toward me to change
subjects, asked if I had a bike.

Said he saw some kids
on Stuyvesant riding badass
10-speed name brands.
I declined. He warned *best to*

want than refuse what's free.
Told me to expect one,
like other kids, on Christmas.

His eyes were clouded, though.
Squinty. He kept blotting his fore-
head with a torn paper towel.
The hand with one finger gone
missing kept scratching, tugging
at his face, his arms, his legs,
where my grandmother's cat,
Camelot, rubbed against
my father's hems revealing
a pair of mismatched socks:
one white with his blood
seeping through the ankle
the other, brown & unclean.

On Real Costs

The real price of every thing, what **every thing** really costs to the man who wants to acquire it, is the toil and trouble of acquiring it. What every thing is really worth to the man who has acquired it, and who wants to dispose of it or exchange it for something else, is the toil and trouble which it can save to himself, and which it can impose upon other people. What **is bought with** money or with goods is purchased by labour as much as what we acquire by the toil of **our** own **body.** That money or those goods indeed save us this **toil.** They contain the value of a certain quantity of labour which we exchange for what **is** supposed at the time to contain the value of an equal quantity. Labour was **the first price,**[.] the original purchase-money that was paid for all things. It was not by gold or by silver, but **by labour,** that all the **we**alth of the world was originally purchased; and its value, to those who possess it, and who want to **exchange** it for some new productions, is precisely equal to the quantity of lab**our** which it can enable them to purchase or command.

Wealth, as Mr Hobbes says, is power. But the person who either acquires, or succeeds to a great fortune, does not necessarily acquire or succeed to any political power, either civil or military. His fortune may, perhaps, afford him the means of acquiring both, but the mere **possess**ion of that fortune does not necessarily convey to him either. The **power** which that possession immediately **and** directly conveys to him, is the power of purchasing a certain command over all labour, or over all the produce of labour which is then in the market. His fortune is greater or less, **precisely** in proportion to the extent of this power; or to the quantity either of other men's labour, or, what is the same thing, of **t**he produce of other men's labour, which it enables him to **purchase** or command. The exchangeable value of every thing must always be precisely equal to the extent of **[the spoils.]** which it conveys to its owner.

'80s Child's Play

Tag?

    No. Touching.

Dodge ball?

    No. Hitting.

Kickball?

    No. Kicking.

Fort?

    No. Darkness.

House?

    Hell. No.

Doctor?

    What kind?

Don't know.

    No.

Plantation?

    I'll kill you.

Duran Duran?

    God. No.

Tongue Kiss?

        Ewww. No.

Dolls?

        Maybe later.

Music?

        No. Dancing.

Biking?

        No bike.

Then what?

        Nothing.

Nothing?

        Quiet.

That's dull.

        Says who?

Me.

        Why?

We're kids.

        I was.

When?

        Once.

The Revolt of Gryllacridadae, The Impoverished

let's assume [you've seen] this critter—half something or other—or you've heard its abdomen thumping against the ground like a steel-toe against a strike plate or felt the flash of its wingspread, when threatened, like how a newly brandished gun makes [quark-sized] men omnipotent.

let's assume you've heard this critter leads a reclusive, which is to say insular, life secreting [balms over] all that's not theirs—that leaf, that glass cage, that gold grill, that color, [that block, that body, that finger]. they will [wrath] over a thumb in their cage. they will draw blood.

let's assume their researcher tries to contain them. they will vault out of their glass. they aren't there [for] science's [whim or ill amusement]. fuck the experiment that put them in this predicament in the first place. they'll jump if injured, or if they are owed—and [they are owed]—or if they are [broken]—and they are ruptured [by one stray nick]—on the lip of their coop, viscera from the thorax. as the entomologists [consuming anguish] race to fix the accident they caused, Gryllacridadae will pause and feast on themselves. taking delight in the fat of their own body, [their spoil], their death, their terms.

Penitence

—Trenton, NJ 1996

my father slips out
of this plane, his eyes shift
to where I sit uncomfortably,
primed for retreat.
AIDS has plaqued his lucidity;
he speaks in nonsense, if at all.

> *Saint Francis, patron of animals*
> *Saint Francis, brother of birds*
> *Saint Francis, mystical seer*
> *charged by the Christ:*
> *"go and repair my house;*
> *it's falling into ruins."*
> *Saint Francis of broken fractals*
> *Saint Francis of mindless guff*
> *Saint Francis of hospitium funk*
> *Saint Francis of vesper and shiv*
> *Saint Francis of dichroic light*

no mirrors in this unit
his social worker, who
earlier called and pled
his terminal case, warns:
glass can be broken and used
as weapons; reflections frustrate.
and, there, under his hospital gown
ink-stamped "property of St. Francis,"
my father,

in a moment of pure
recall, says: *aye, boy, I know*
I owe you a bike, right? laughing
toothless and soft, *a nigga's*
a little late. you forgive me?

$y = 2x - 1$

For this to work, the variables must
share an origin, a known relationship.
When coordinates are located,
y can be solved to form an arrow—
fine Cartesian line compressing Euclidean time
& space—

the shortest distance
between two points on a flat surface.

Though, nothing of substance is flat,
is it? Euclid didn't know the earth
was cambered & curved outward
& in. All he must have known,
sitting in Plato's Academy in Athens,
was that somewhere a lover waited
for him to reach a certain endpoint.

But suppose Euclid died before
he arrived home, his lover still waiting.
His body would appear mere inches from a caress—
a straight line away from all he could have had,
had he not been bridging distances, drawing lines,
solving why
on paper.

O Father, Who All in Heaven?

Men stuck between camel humps,
hollow be their name. Hard-willed,
undone on earth but not in heaven.
They, too, are given their daily bread.
Wayward who roved where spirit ain't
are forgiven for their trespass as I
have forgiven myself for imagining
chaos. Libertines with iron anchors
held in their good hand are delivered
forever and ever from the glory
circus that powers whosoever
labors least. While the journeymen,
pockets full of stone, enter the river
praising death as long-lost son, or savior.

On Debt

In a com-
mercial country **abounding**
with every sort of expensive luxury, the sovereign,
in the same manner as almost all the great · proprietors in his
dominions, naturally spends a great part of his revenue in purchasing
those luxuries. His own and the neighbouring countries supply
him abundantly with all the costly trinkets which compose the
splendid but insignificant pageantry of a court. For the sake of an
inferior pageantry of the same kind, his nobles dismiss their retainers,
make their tenants independent, and become **gradually** themselves
as insignificant as the greater part of the wealthy burghers in
his dominions. The same frivolous passions which influence their
conduct influence his. How can it be supposed that he should be the
only rich man in his dominions who is insensible to pleasures of this
kind? If he does not, what he is very likely to do, spend upon those
pleasures so great a part of his revenue as **debilitate[s]** very much the
defensive power of the state, it cannot well be expected that he
should not spend upon them all that part of it which is over and
above what is necessary for supporting that **defensive power.** His
ordinary expense becomes equal to his ordinary revenue, and it is
well if it does not frequently exceed it. The amassing of **treasure can**
no longer be expected [.] and when extraordinary exigencies
require extraordinary expenses, he must necessarily call upon his
subjects for an extraordinary aid. **The present and the late** king of
Prussia are the only great princes of Europe who, since the death of
Henry IV of France in 1610, are supposed to have amassed any con-
siderable treasure. The parsimony which leads to **accumulation**
[becomes] almost as rare in republican as in monarchical governments.
The Italian republics, the United Provinces of the Netherlands,
are all in debt. The canton of Berne is the single republic in
Europe which has amassed **a**ny **considerable [archive,]** The other
Swiss republics have not. The taste for some sort of pageantry, for
splendid buildings, at least, and other public ornaments, frequently
prevails as much in the apparently sober senate-house of a little
republic as in the dissipated court of the greatest king. The want of
parsimony in time of peace imposes the necessity of contracting
debt in time of war. When war comes, there is no money in the treasury
but what is necessary for carrying on [?] the ordinary expense
of the peace establishment. In war an establishment of three or four
times that expense becomes necessary for the defence of the state,
and consequently a revenue three or four times greater than the
peace revenue.

PTSD

Paralysis

What seems like a simple suggestion—"Miss, could you move up in the line please . . . ?"—becomes so much more complicated for someone like me. Indecisive. Afraid to take the plunge. Like the time my friends invited me to skinny dip in the river behind their house. It was autumn, too chilly, too damp. I promised I would but instead sat frozen on the hem of the shore, shivering, dressed appropriately enough for high noon but too scantily for post-twilight briskness. I wasn't one of those bare, thick-skinned souls who frolicked in cold water. Point is, I get invited to parties and never show up. It's not that I don't want to go, but that I stand on the threshold contemplating what I'd do if I stayed home: Write a poem, binge a drama, refuse to call my mother, write a letter to my congressman about some issue I haven't taken the time to understand, stand fifteen goddamn minutes in the doorway deciding something else.

Therapist

My therapist said *make one decision and document it* I told her if I could I wouldn't need therapy She asked why I was so resistant to commitment I couldn't decide I don't like people to expect I don't like to expect Too many people expect All of these reasons None of them She implored *tell me a story of the first decision you ever made and didn't regret* I couldn't decide and settled for this:

Stress Disorder

in 1979 after OPEC raised the price of oil/my father cuffed the hem of his pants and handed me a needle/for the drug addict to have someone else shoot them up is a sacred intimacy—on par with sex—he had blown all his veins except those in the hard-to-reach areas/the one behind his knee/he taught me how to position the needle and not panic when it turned red—that blood was sacred like communion wine/*push down on the plunger . . . slowly . . . push . . . release*/and i had a choice/shoot him up or suffer worse i plunged/blood inched up the barrel/

he shook/i wept/he nodded/i slept/

the both of us
resting in a distant
cousin to peace.

elegy for the moaner, 2016

After 20 years of gathering dust, it's time
to remove the urn from the cabinet
and put him beneath proper ground.
There's the small problem of not having
a pine box for the body made
smaller by not having his body at all.

Hell, I don't have a choir to sing riffs
and not one pastor to eulogize.
I abandoned hat feathers and black
church theatrics to settle on myrrh
kindling and mindful mantras.
Although I concede: burials should be
an occasion of final rites, pomp
and happenstance, if you will,
with at least one moaner who may or
may not miss the departed. And so
I gather alone

with a shovel in my backyard
and his needle in my forethought.
I offer earth what I have—these brick pavers,
his cheap urn, the memory of my sister's
fist through our front door window
and the gentle way he sobered to wrap
her paw in an old shirt. The tin lunchbox
in which he, high, captured the rabid
bat that bit me while I slept.
Except it wasn't a bat at all, but a wren—
imagine a grown man chasing a bird
just to say he finally caught something
elusive. Thankfully, that bat spell took.
The bird flew. We fled. I lived.

We all lived for a while at least
until we didn't. I am now miles
from where he spoke his last words:
Even God left. I'm only . . .

Understood. If the reaper RSVPs,
men wait at the forked road
with fresh baked chaff
grown over many summers—
bounty cut lovely, dross shot up.
Fool hands won't notice Lucifer
manages the silo, his barters larcenous.

I once loathed the blind risks
that made men harvest pulse and
bet full stalk. Laid odds against gains
and harbored spite of ill gambles.
But loss humbles, hindsight mellows,
since my double down with rage
                never once paid—
never once raised
                my father from any grave.

Positive Curvature

No story can be told straight

on spheres like earth; lines bulge.

The shortest distance is measured in circles, rays

bowed out, hourglassed & spiraled

like wheel tracks in desert sand

made by who knows who. Let's say,

some desperate man is trapped in Death

Valley on the unicycle he promised

his 11-year-old, one summer, many years ago.

While navigating hills, dunes, saddles

& mirage, he must juggle & cycle

straight ahead, follow his heart, ignore

compulsion & turn neither left nor right.

In due time, he will find his daughter,

older & smiling at the border of that desert.

Should she look across sands at her father's journey,

she'll notice his path winding, circuitous;

yet, somehow, calculably brief & inevitable.

etymology

because my mother named me after a child   borne still
to a godmother I've never met   I took another way to be
known   something easier to remember   inevitable
to forget   something that rolls over the surface of thrush
because   I grew tired of saying
no it's pronounced . . .   now I tire of not
conjuring that ghost I honor   say it with me: Airea
rhymes with sarah
sarah from the latin meaning   a woman of high rank
which also means whenever I ask anyone to hold me
on their lips   I sound like what I almost am

hear me out: I'm not a Dee   or a river
charging through working-class towns where union folk
cogwedge for plots   & barely any house at all
where bosses mangle ethnic phonemes & nobody   corrects one
word because the check's in the mail   so let's end
this classist pretence   where names don't matter
& language is too heavy a lift   my e is silent
like most people should be
the consonant is sonorant
is a Black woman   or one might say the spine

I translate to "wind" in a country known for its iron
imply "lioness of God"   in Jesus's tongue
mean "apex predator"   free of known enemy
fierce enough to harm   or fast enough to run
all I'm saying is   what I've already said:

the tongue has no wings   to flee what syllables it fears
the mouth is no womb   has no right to consume   what it did not make

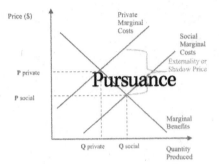

Each individual commodity fights for itself. . . . The spectacle is the epic poem of this struggle. . . .

—Guy Debord

We Was Kings

Been trying to show you history
don't change much. There's hard proof
erasure repeats. What we learn to accept
are tidy myths full of men who look unlike
me. Still people, but not my dad or my uncle
who would share stories about a line of black
kings in Scotland. How in 967, Dubh the Black,
son of Malcolm, was called Vehement Niger.
Dubh was driven from the field by his cousin,
Cullen, next in line. How that king was offed
by Dubh's brother, Kenneth, who looked a lot
like Obama, if Obama lived in Kirkcaldy
in the late 900s. Even then, brothers wilded
out in a country that found it suitable to call
their kings niggers. This went on until every
mudtongue fisher of sweet bone bread ground
to chalk. Until the new kings with lighter eyes
and narrow features commissioned portraits
in which every past heir had a porcelain face,
only the backgrounds had any dark. All those
kings, who looked familiar, wading as muted
novas in a celestial sea of utter blankness.

On Mobility

The whole value of **the seed**, too, is properly a fixed capital. Though it goes backwards and forwards between the ground and granary, it never **changes master**s, and therefore does not properly circulate. The farmer makes his profit, not by its sale, but **by its increase**. The general stock of any country or society is the same as that of all its inhabitants or members, and therefore naturally divides itself into the same three portions, each of which has a distinct function or office. The first is that portion which is reserved for immediate consumption, **and** of which the characteristic is, that it affords no revenue or profit. It **consists** in the stock **of [fine] food,** clothes, furniture, &c. which have been purchased by their proper consumers, but which are not yet entirely consumed. The whole stock of mere **dwelling-houses,** too, subsisting at any one time in the country, make a part of this first portion. . . . A dwelling-house, as such, contributes nothing to the revenue of its inhabitant; and although it is, no doubt, extremely useful to him, it is as his clothes and household **furniture[,]** are useful to him, which, however, makes a part of his expense, and not of his revenue. If it is to be let to a tenant for rent, as the house itself can produce nothing, the tenant must always pay the rent out of some other revenue which he derives either from labour, or **stock,** or land. Though a house, therefore, may yield a revenue to its proprietor, and thereby serve in the function of a capital to him, it cannot yield any to the public, nor serve in the function of a **capital[,]** to it, and the revenue of the whole body of the people can never be in the smallest degree increased by it. . . . In countries where masquerades are common, it is a trade to let out **masquerade dresses[,]** for a night. Upholsterers frequently let furniture by the month or by the year. Undertakers let the furniture of funerals by the day **and** by the week. **many people** let furnished houses, and get a rent, not only for the use of the house, **but** for that of the furniture. The revenue, however, which **is** derived from such things must always be ultimately drawn from some other source of revenue. Of all parts of the stock, either of an individual, or of a society, reserved for immediate consumption, what is laid out in houses is **most slowly consumed.**

Kafkaesque

The real hero in *The Metamorphosis* was Grete, Gregor's sister, who
found a way to avoid the snares. Who wants to deliver spoiled milk
to a roach every morning? Right now, there's a mouse in my kitchen.
I've set down poison, but he's too wise. Whatever he wants, he'll
substitute. He can wait for his French Revolution. The guillotine
tomorrow. Or, maybe, there's enough to form a union or maybe they
decided when their Hoffa disappeared, they didn't want any more
smoke. I figure I'm the FBI to Stuart Little's mafia. They know when
I am trying to frame them. They slink around those traps. Find
cheese laughable. They get thick on Kool-Aid crystals sunken into
the grout. Prefer what's sweet to what's savory. They know what
they want. Smarter than most. See, my desires fleet. But I'll Pavlov
dog it every time. Ring the bell. Give me a shock. Ring the bell. Give
me a scrap. Ring the bell. I'll stinkbug it. Will fly to a new wall to
meet the same end. Crushed by habit. But let's not delve into the
mechanics of what's slowly killing me. Today I'm trying
to end this pestilence, and these pests,
at least, know not to fall for the same trap twice.

American Ouroborus

i've been an imaginary

a mandala gone wrong

& a mascot unmasked

even been a star-draped snake

consuming my own tail

feting the spectacle

in rituals of self-worship

as freedom unravels

the pornotrope prances

& who speaks of this country

slithering as the American Way

driven to every brink

wheeled by certain cognitive error

inherent in rhetorical stutter

& ego's steepled needs

such suffering portends

grave danger ever awaits

patriots who liquor a hearth fire & renegades who gather for warmth

as their brothers strike a match   in a house swiftly filling with gas

-Icity

—for

January 2004–December 2012

Cyclicity (n.) the quality or state of being cyclic, as in: At the age of 13, after a brutal ripping, ██████████ told the court, *I'd rather be dead.* A little more than a decade later, the 23-year-old mother hollowed her 8-year-old daughter in front of her other four children with a secondhand Salvation Army bread knife. The crime, reported at 2:30 a.m., occurred in the kitchen. She claims her daughter, ██████, was making a sandwich and the doorbell rang. Everything happened so fast, so fast. At the scene, police reported her breath smelled of metabolizing alcohol. The house was unkempt, kitchen counter strewn with burnt tin foil, shelves bare except for mayonnaise. When the police questioned why there was no other evidence of a sandwich, the mother reached for the bloody knife on top of her refrigerator, pointed to her daughter's lifeless body on the floor, and screamed, *DON'T YOU SEE ALL THAT BREAD?*

Basicity (n.) of or relating to a base or starting point, as in: Back in 2000, ██████ wrote a letter for the family judge deciding her guardianship, *People think I'm crazy because of things I do and I might need help because these streets thieve off sweet.* When the process server issued a personal summons to ██████'s mother, adjuring her to obtain her troubled teenaged daughter, ██████ cracked the door, *I DON'T HAVE TIME TO DEAL WITH HER RIGHT NOW.* ██████ slammed the door. ██████ turned up Earth, Wind & Fire. ██████ closed her blinds.

Causticity (n.) capable of destroying or eating away by chemical action, as in: Many heroin users seek a high to ease the effects of the gully. The poor man's Prozac. Heroin is often the drug of choice for sex workers and schizophrenics. In high doses, users float in a dreamlike state, alienated from all that drove the needle. Addicts will doze off, unaware, after a fix. Veins will give in, collapse. Muscling begins. Dense fibers twitch causing bruising, blooming skin, abscesses, and infections. At the scene, police noticed the 23-year-old mother drifting in and out of sleep, while standing. One officer noted purple marks under her skin, tentacled tracks down her arms, two blank black eyes.

Chronicity (n.) marked by long duration or frequent recurrence, as in: ████████████ would leave her four children with extended family for long periods. She said she was running to work and would be right back. Relatives report she was a prostitute and would pick up the children days or weeks later. The Division of Youth and Family Services intervened on numerous occasions, including January 2004 when ██████ was born cocaine-addicted. ████████████, █████'s grandmother, assumed temporary custody. Over the years, the four children were placed in foster homes—repeatedly—but always returned to their mother. In November 2012, ██████ was found with bite marks on her arms, legs, and torso. She told her teacher, *MOMMY DID IT*. One month after her death, ██████'s younger brother disclosed, *MOMMY TRIED TO KILL US A LOT, 'SPECIALLY* ████.

Synchronicity (n.) the experiences of two or more events as meaningfully related, where they are unlikely to be causally related, as in: Two nights before ██████ was killed, I dreamt of a haunted doll with three symmetrical holes where her heart would have been. Slumped, she sat buttering her forearm with her chin, at one end of a carved table in a city's empty cafeteria. I was opposite of her, knitting the sweater I was wearing. A clock, out of view, chimed. She stood and walked toward me, a tureen on the flat of her palm. As she neared, she used her teeth to open the lid—countless disembodied eyes. Some crimson, some burnt umber, some crossed, some blacked, all blinking dim marble. She handed me the dish, imploring,

FEED OUR GUESTS
SO THEY'LL SEE
HOW I TASTE.

Logical Disjunction

Either the queen is dead or
she crowns your hand

Either your fathers were kings or
they died homeless paupers

Either your mother is a nigga nigga or
she's a half-white nigga

Either race is a genetic experiment or
it's a ransacked Section 8

Either humans use their claws or
humans are consumed

Either history stutters or
history was born mute

Either paradise is a congress of hoes or
hell's rivers have no mouths

Either someone holds a mirror or
someone else has no reflection

Either "they" means alla them there or
"we" means alla us here

Either this is a free country or
the dream is wildly overpriced

Either hoard is fear misspelled or
lack is hoard's synonym

Either broke men leave nothing or
nothing breaks death's weight

Either you wail ENOUGH into space and
it is emptied breath inside an urn or
it is hurricane to dust.

The Broke Diet

My friend, who I called my best friend, died in July. Many Julys ago. His body was discovered in a motel on the fringe of Detroit's downtown corridor. He was found exceedingly dead, hemorrhaging from his ears, blood on his pillow, mouth open and his computer gone. While my best friend, who had many best friends, struggled with a history of heroin use, his best friend had a history of savior complex. We were a pair. Either way, I never forgot how he went shopping with borrowed money to make a meal for my family after the birth of my daughter. He seemed healthy then. I was sure that he'd quit cold, but addictions have a way of warming white knuckles.

Some summers past, we were at a midtown sushi restaurant talking about what we wanted to be when we grew up. We were both grown. I noticed that he lost weight, asked whether he ate regularly. He said, "This that broke diet." We laughed. In the slow months after touring with his band, he would take off to New York and busk in subway tunnels—he needed a little something to help with the bills and edge the hunger. I never thought to ask if the subway was a metaphor. I didn't bother to spy his fingertips. Didn't have him roll up his sleeve.

My best friend, who had many best friends, once serenaded me with a cover of Stevie Wonder's "As" in the parking lot of Union Street Diner. He was the friend whose calls I always answered. We last talked about writing secrets. Shortly after, he devoured a snowball—a mix of heroin and crack. Crack speeds. Heroin slows. His heart resisted, ballooning to burst.

And even though you knew just what was coming
you were so damned tired of running

My friend, who I called my best friend, wrote those song lyrics before he died. He was an honest prophet of sorts who loved only men but had fucked a woman here and there. He lived his own unbound truth. He didn't care about marriage of any kind—"marriage is too straight" he once told me. He wasn't concerned with the geometry of congruent lines. He wanted to swirl into space on his own trajectory. And I suspect in his last few minutes, in that funk-infested midden where he was using with another of his best friends, that's exactly what he did—spiral in sync to his own EKG.

All the best friends decided to cover up his actual cause of death. Nobody needed to know about the shooting up, the lying, the trap house hangouts, and derelict other best friends. We warped a believable yarn. He rented a cheap room for the air-conditioning and succumbed to heatstroke in the middle of the night. That was the weave. He died having a multitude of best friends who adored knowing him, and, yet, in our shame-fucked logic, we thought it more honorable to be memorialized as a man who died from heat in a food desert rather than snow in an avalanche.

The Rules of Attention

Sunlight barges through our windows, lands across
my cheek, forceful as a slap. I place my morning
news down, sorrowed by some other mother's loss,
some other mother's loves not returning home
how they left. Wrong place, wrong minute, wrong

               color, wrong body. As if any of those things signify. I tell my sons
the problem with time is the separate rules for observing it, which is not to say
every moment doesn't have meaning, which is to say every second is a lesson.
What matters is knowing the distance between

               a wink and a blink, what harms and what suggests harm, a vari-
ance measured in milliseconds. Knowing, too, if, at any given instant, you
are seen through a smudged lens as innocuous object

  or armament
fantasy beheld
    or flesh
      to be torn asunder.

Debord's Deconstructed Spectacle, Before

In societies where **modern conditions** of production prevail, life is **present**ed as an **immense** accumulation of **spectacles.** Everything that was directly lived has receded **in**to a representation. **T**he **i**mage**s** detached from every aspect of life merge into a common stream in which the unity of that life can no longer be recovered. **fragmented** views of reality regroup themselves into a new unity as a separate pseudo-**world** that can only be looked at. The specialization of images of the world has culminated in a world of autonomized images where **even** the **deceivers are deceived.** The spectacle is a concrete inversion of life, an autonomous movement of the nonliving. The spectacle presents itself simultaneously as society itself, as a part of society, and as a *means of unification.* As a part of **society['s]**, it is ostensibly the focal point of all vision and all consciousness: But due to the very fact that this sector is *separate*, it is in reality the domain of **delusion** and false consciousness: the unification it **achieves** is **nothing but** an official language of **universal separation[;]**. The spectacle is not a collection of images; it is a social relation between **people** that is mediated by images. The spectacle cannot be **understood as** a **mere** visual excess produced by mass-media technologies. It is a world-view that has actually been materialized, that has become an objective reality. Understood in its totality, the spectacle is both the result and the project of the present mode of **product**ion. It is not a mere supplement **or decoration[.]**added to the real world, it is **the heart** of this real society's unreality. In all of its particular manifestations—news, propaganda, advertising, entertainment—the spectacle is the *model* of the prevailing way of life. It is the omni-present affirmation of the choices that have *already been made* in the sphere of production and in the consumption implied by that production. In both form and content the spectacle serves as a total justification **of** the conditions and goals of the existing system. The spectacle is also the *constant* **presence** of this justifi-cation since it monopolizes the majority of the time spent outside the modern production process. Separation is itself an integral part of the unity of this world, of a global social praxis **split into reality** **and** **image.**

Cost of the Floss

In 1981, my mother, sister, and I fled my first home with only the clothes on our backs. Unhomed for a time, we eventually moved to a small working-class suburb—a bridge and state away. Good public schools. Decent class size. Nary another Black kid. We struggled differently—not for breath but for being.

We made certain choices while others were made for us. We indulged and went without. My family didn't even own a couch until I was thirteen. In lieu of a Chesterfield, we had a queen-sized mattress in the living room. We lived, ate, and slept on the floor. Played hard games of Scrabble while watching *The Jeffersons*. That was our good life on the Serta.

I made it a point, however, to avoid bringing friends to our apartment. As a Black kid who desperately wanted to fit the suburban mold, explaining a mattress in the middle of the living room floor to kids with fully furnished homes was too daunting and personal. Seriously, how do you explain owning seven pairs of Jordache jeans, a gold rope chain, and the freshest shelltoe Adidas with fat laces, while drinking from free-with-purchase McDonald's cups in a bare apartment?

I'd visited my friends' houses. Sat on their parents' flowered sofas, fragrant with ointment, hard salami, and Love's Baby Soft. Ate Beefaroni for supper at their dining room tables and peeked into their mothers' dust-hazed bowls. Saw the well-matched bathroom towels, the French Provincial headboards, and Rob Lowe torn from the pages of *Teen Beat*. The last thing I wanted was to be judged or have allegations of poverty thrown into the othering stew. I resisted any scenario that would give rise to those events. Instead, I asked for things I knew my mother couldn't afford, then boasted about the newest acquisition to whoever would listen. The façade of conspicuous consumption was both sanctuary and armor.

Time's subjective eraser allowed me to forget all about my young blush and floss until a few years ago. Driving toward some immemorable place, I noticed a silver hazmat suit in a vintage store window. I swerved across two lanes of traffic to park outside this store I'd frequently never visited. I wasn't in the market for a potentially radioactive textile, but the strange past has my number.

I like what I like—outmoded tchotchkes, things in conflict with the color of expectation.

I grabbed my leather satchel from the passenger seat and fed a meter three quarters while readying myself with the pregnant possibility of stuffing that metallic getup with cotton batting and turning it into a robotic scarecrow to ward off the squirrel-thugs in my front yard. Not to mention the hearts and attention I would garner on social media when I posted my wondrous creation. The thought of my spacecrow in a Ludwig filter quickened my step!

Immediately upon entering the store, I was transported to the '70s with its plastic-laminate furniture and gold-plated clocks with sharp rays circling the frame. I stared at the tarnished rays, lost in the memory of a wall with one of those same clocks on it. Maybe it was in my first home, but that was unlikely since my family couldn't afford the '70s until 1989.

A woman with a Northern Michigan accent interrupted my time travel by asking, "May I help you find something in particular?"

"Yes, how much is the hazmat suit in the window?"

"It's quite expensive. In fact, I'm not even sure it's still for sale. Let me check."

I knew this routine all too well—the *Assume-Black-Means-Broke* downsell.

She sauntered toward the cash register to confirm the price. I climbed across two dark walnut coffee tables and straddled a porcelain lamp with a carved face of Marie Antoinette to check the price myself. I turned the tag over, spied the numbers 5-8-5, and gasped "Oh, hell no!" I climbed back over the tables, slid on a pile of *LIFE* magazines, and waited for the clerk to return.

"Suit's $585," she trumpeted. "Real deal, too."

"I can tell. That's authentic . . . waste . . . protection." I lied aloud like I had *Antiques Roadshow*-level knowledge of the vintage hazmat suit market.

"Not too much, then?"

"Of course not! It's practically free. I just want to see what else catches my eye. Let me look around."

And that's what I did. I thoughtfully looked around as my leather satchel brushed up against hideous wicker lamps, useless rooster figurines, and purposely knocked over Mammy bric-a-brac in the '50s kitchen section. And at every turn, that clerk shadowed me so closely she could number my pulse. Surely, she assumed I would five-finger discount some worthless gimcrack that nobody needed then any more than we needed it now.

After three very deliberate rounds on the floor and tiring of surveillance, I turned back and instructed "Wrap up the suit." She disappeared behind a large stack of 35mm reels to ring up my order, her face hinting smug relief.

As my credit card scraped through their reader, a soft white hipster couple approached the register. They inquired about the price of a print with Warhol and Basquiat in boxing gloves. In that Northern Michigan accent, the clerk said, "I don't know if that's for sale. I do know it's quite expensive."

Blood coursed from my head to the tips of my fingers. I now noticed the No Returns/No Refunds sign. I furiously remembered flowered sofas, crystal bowls, McDonald's glasses, and the living room mattress of my youth. There I was again, willing to prove to someone who doesn't know me that I could afford to shatter their perception. My motivations to floss quickly unraveled to reveal my threadbare 1984 veil, and the only thing missing was my well-scripted shame: "Yeah, I, like, can't have friends over when my mom isn't home/isn't feeling well/is working/has a headache/(is depressed and watching TV on the living room mattress)."

I still haven't purchased cotton batting nor figured out how to make my spacecrow stand erect without an advanced degree in engineering. It's a sloppy fold on my garage shelf. And, with one of the mechanical doors busted, squirrels chew off pieces of the hazmat suit to pad their slipshod dreys. At the sightline of the barest elm's tightest branch, their nests emerge highly visible, out in the open, for all to envy the shameless comfort of having nothing to prove.

Making an Essential Nigga

—for the Stockholders

Make famous at most two
Of any of these niggas:
Nigga ain't got shit nigga
Think they ain't shit nigga
Circle jerk, eye jizzed nigga
Jeans slung low nigga
Bespoke ass nigga
Stellar CV nigga
Made for TV nigga
Hamhock potlicka nigga
Grease that scalp nigga
Pimp that pain nigga
Ain't I pretty nigga
Wave cap, boar brush nigga
Milk & toast milquetoast nigga
Got invited & I went nigga
Kingmaker-led nigga
Traffic signal trigga nigga
On the map nigga
GPS to the grave nigga
30 and a crown now nigga
Captain Sunk can't swim nigga
Don't make no waves nigga
Sharks worse than whips nigga
Cotton gin boom nigga
Wait for that gavel nigga
Going once, going twice
Sold to the highest bidda nigga
Massa sho good to me nigga
Ampersand & asterisk nigga
Spade, hoe, & dibber nigga
Hard red winter nigga
Phenom funambulist nigga

Credit to the race nigga
Please, Sir, call me nigga nigga
Spring white soft baked nigga
Somebody gotta get it nigga
If not me then who nigga
Now you see me nigga
Now you don't nigga
What's your name nigga
Should I know you nigga
Aren't you that other nigger nigga
You look like that other nigger nigga
Nobody told you nigga
You're revision history nigga
Yousa ripped page nigga
Yousa dog ear nigga
Yousa footnote nigga
Yousa if then nigga
If that nigga
If that

Barnum & Bailey's Word Problem for the Come Up

If all born from two flugelhorns tweet about fungible crypto & pleiaidians clock at 5 p.m. gross nationally & someone on a hilltop has an invariable cry surrounded by a bank of locusts & nudefoot Franklins unruche to winnow exponentially & shadows bull & brutes bear & pilgrims die at the borrowed edge of regret & winter is red & summer is black & gussied up pigeons are profiting as doves & soulsick is just long division in drag & all awake aren't well or invested & for two pennies more a half-coded avatar will haggle dry your saltwater bread & tease inverted nipples for a rattail comb—aren't you excited now & don't you want it insured & don't you want this return to compound harder & if liquid, at what rate will Annie Asset make it rain?

Meeting Wittgenstein at the Circus

Summer of 2014. I bought tickets for the Universoul Circus. A family perfor-
mance, a reclamation: a black-on-black gaze with Brazilian contortionists,
Trinidadian dancers, Ghanaian tamers. After locating a parking space near the
main road, my two older boys darted out of my truck while my two younger kids
grabbed my hands. As I shifted my shoulders to settle the contents of my back-
pack, a Ford F-150 blasting Lynyrd Skynyrd slowed down. Two sandy-haired
boys poked their heads out of the windows to shout "Nigger! Nigger! Nigger!"
Then, the two sped off and left a trail of exhaust over a lush field of wildflowers.

Startled, I looked around. All of us regular folks, who'd paid to see a woman
dislocate her right leg over her head on a Sunday afternoon, hid our disgust.
We disguised our long-simmering anger as ambivalence and inched clan-like
toward the entrance. After the F-150 dispersed into the clouds, a nearby teen
confessed to another, "Nigga, those white boys from our school!" They laughed.
Relatively unaffected, those of us in line reached for our tickets.

My daughter, then a 4-year-old interrogator, tugged on my sleeve.

"Mommy, what's a nigger?"

My thoughts stumbled as I hoped to construct some simple explanation, but
something more complex was at play. Essentially, my kid was asking the ques-
tion the public keeps asking: Why does the word *nigger/a* land differently from
different mouths?

Language is a slick motherfucker—a gabardine devil to the left or the gossamer
wing to the right narrating the texture of our lives. And yet only a detail-oriented
few ever bother to wonder how the winged devil shapes our world and thoughts.

Under the tutelage of Bertrand Russell, Ludwig Wittgenstein wrote *Tractatus
Logico-Philosophicus* and posited that language represents the world through
depiction, and pictures are how we think through and process material cul-
ture. Essentially, the white boys, who hurled the word "nigger" across a field,
held a racist and distorted representation of what a *nigger* looks like or how

a *nigger* acts. Steeped in myth, historical bias, and racial conflation, a *nigger* becomes synonymous with a black space where nothing true is seen and all nuance is invisible. In the mouths of those boys, the word was meant to enforce a projection—a caricature devoid of value, a body unseen, a haint, a specter. Which leads to the critical questions: if the body is invisible, does it exist? Can it be pained?

Later in his career, Wittgenstein discarded much of what he'd earlier argued by moving away from the picture theory to a "tool" theory. Pictures, after all, convey an object, while tools have many uses. Believing now that the strength of words derives from a series of intersecting similarities, Wittgenstein advocated instead for purposeful connections and resemblances. Meaning, with its own set of conventions and rules, is subjugated to use in this "language game." Framed in Wittgenstein's signature aphoristic style, he insists that we don't ask for the meaning of the word; we ask for the use. This scaffolding helps to explain the Black teens and their adaptation of the word.

When one is called a *nigger*, a received "fact" is being imposed. But when one calls themself a *nigga*, it can be viewed as intentional nonsense, a disruption of historical weight, or a term of endearment. All are allowed in the language game because, according to Wittgenstein, we are all constantly operating inside of language with agency. No longer are words an imposition or enacted on us. The rules are subject to our evaluations and assignment of meaning; we have an actual say. We determine how the word is used, if the word is used, and when it's deployed properly.

Like deeds, words are concerted actions eliciting visceral responses. They conjure images. And we, fragile and human neophytes, have been given responsibility for these menacing weapons. We dodge and flex however we've been conditioned, contort in the ways our forebears have taught us.

With these ideas loosely in mind, a spotlight cast on a single tightrope. I respond to my daughter's question: "*Nigger* is an acrobat, a word with double joints."

Without skipping a rapt beat, she settled back into her seat, countered, "Oh . . . I thought niggas were flowers."

Cirque du Sims

In this carnival clowns cluster
inside the ringmaster's imagining.
They're woke and tired. Oppose GMOs
& don't know why, eat vegan & have
luxury beef. Love whoever they want
& ghost whoever they don't. Act brand-
new whenever they act. Always.

Act. Take copious selfies to recall
what they look like through
a filter, in a visually fortuitous
moment. Say: *wait let me*
video this present suffering.
Gather followers like sheep
flocks who envy how plastic
their bending, how full-on
their fake. First tooth babies
they crowned or borrowed for
promise of other's pleasure.

These vote incapable tickets,
pay taxes or don't, drive
electric or synthetic,
tattoo fylfots, foe for friends,
double lens this or that, flip,
flop, hard knuckle dead ends,
abolish the hood to free up
the market, tar & feather
difference, execute nuance
on the wheel, townsquare
their public beheadings, or
McCarthy their cancellations
while basking, fallible, under
shine of the spotlight divine.

The Ancestors School a Basic Bitch

We're saying we're exhausted

by you. Coveting the smallest sliver

of attention just so you might feel

requisite a little while longer,

a little more desirable to nobodies.

Bodies don't even matter. Do you

listen to the signs we send—

beetles in the crux of storm, stray

pussies meowing you home, June

bed defiled by mice? And you

fancy yourself a goddess for no earthly

reason. Think of how fiercely Persephone

unyoked March from May. Recall Inanna

had enough sense to visit Hell and not

reminisce the landscape.

O' S*^#! Shakespeare Dropping 'Net Knowledge

Renewed some mother's o'er blest womb
Turn the black bile 'round the tomb
Pluck the glass eye of her prime
Wrinkle now her auric time
Feast the image men engrave
Walk the cobbled, weedy pave
Mint the brow into the field
Until the mist to chill does yield.
The stagnant moss inside the quay
Was once the ivy of its day
And we, who blest, do age beyond
The dumb of youth and its blank pond
Will find a truth that we once feared:
We cleave to all that wanes each year.

O Pleas

There is one sort of **labour** which adds to the value of the **subject** upon which it is bestowed: There is another which has no such **effect**. The former, as it produces a value, may be called productive; the latter, unproductive labour. Thus the labour of a **manufacturer** adds, generally, to the value of the **materials** which he works upon, that of his own maintenance, and of his master's **profit**. The labour of a **menial** servant, on the contrary, adds to the value of nothing. Though the manufacturer has his wages advanced to him by his master, he, in reality, costs him no **expence**, the value of those wages being **general**ly restored, together with a profit, in the improved value of the subject upon which his labour is bestowed. But the maintenance of a menial **servant** never is restored. A **man** grows **rich** by employing a multitude of manufacturers: he grows **poor** by maintaining ' a multitude of menial servants. The labour of the latter, however, has its value, and deserves its reward as well as that of the former. But the labour of the manufacturer fixes and realizes itself in s**o**me **particular** subject or **vendible** commodity, which lasts for some time at least after that labour is past. It is, as it were, a certain quantity of labour stocked and stored up to be employed, if necessary, upon some **o**ther **occasion**. That subject, or what is the same thing, the price of that subject, can afterwards, if necessary, put into motion a quantity of labour equal to that which had originally produced it. The labour of the menial servant, **o**n the **contrary**, does not fix or realize itself in any particular subject or **commodity**. His services generally perish in the very instant of their performance, and seld**o**m leave any **trace** or value behind them for which an equal quantity of service could afterwards be procured

The labour of some of the most re**[spectacle]** orders in the society is, like that of menial servants, unproductive of any value, and does not fix or realize itself in any permanent subject, or vend-**ible** commodity, which endures after that labour is past, and for which an equal quantity of labour could afterwards be procured. The **sovereign**, for example, with all the officers both of justice and war who serve under him, the whole army and navy, are unproductive labourers.... Their service, how honourable, how useful, or how necessary soever, produces **not**hing for which an equal quantity of service can afterwards be procured. The protection, security, and defence of the commonwealth, the effect of their labour this year, will not purchase its protection, security, and defence, for the year to come. In the same class must be ranked, some both of the gravest and most important, and some of the most frivolous professions: churchmen, lawyers, physicians, men of letters of all kinds; **players**, musicians, op**e**ra-singers, **buffoons**, opera-dancers, &c. The labour of the meanest of these has a certain value, regulated by the very same principles which regulate that of every other sort of labour; and that of the **no**blest and most useful, produces nothing which could afterwards **purchased** or procure an equal quantity of labour. Like the declaration of the actor, or the hara**n**gue of the **or**ator, or the tune of the musician, the work of all of them **[sold]**

to tell you three things on my mind is to tell you about quarantine and temperance

a white mentor who i once liked said ". . . good you have four kids. you can spare one." according to *Oxford English Dictionary* the verb *spare* means *afford to give up. to sacrifice.* like time. how we lose ourselves in infinite scroll. lost lifetimes because noon is conceptual. no rhythms. loss is why casinos have no clocks or windows. time is never up in isolation. the evening news clips humpbacks harmonizing. did you know whalespeak sounds like a monastic chant, like a mourning song? and if whales are mourning, who soothes them? certainly not the lantern   nymphs.   they're   busy eating fruit trees. grapevines. and who will ready Sky Daddy's altar come Armageddon? bars been closed for a year. sober sinners, the whole of us ready to erupt, won't be redeemed from a dry land.

the de-vegetated plain on youtube, the place i go to be outside, shows beasts running aimlessly. laminated ferns and extruded wood strangely waste inside zoo enclosures, where the hippos are trying unsuccessfully to drown themselves. too thick skinned. too effective at float. too able to survive. i relate. read the four horsemen soon come after wrangling sick wheat. any moment now. you'll see. Sky Daddy is waiting to unleash. she waiting. WAITING on that one animal to do one more goddamn thing to some animal who has had it up to . . . WAITING . . . a person i've never met explains things i already know . . . WAITING . . . i give doubt vouchers until benefit bursts and p   r   e   g   n   a   n   t

scrolls   unseal   and   god   damn the   language   of   sparing.   i have none to spare. i'm cash poor when it comes to birth. my riches, a wombless sill with seven trumpets and a name holding back four winds WAITING   and   ready   to   blow.

Debord's Deconstructed Spectacle, After

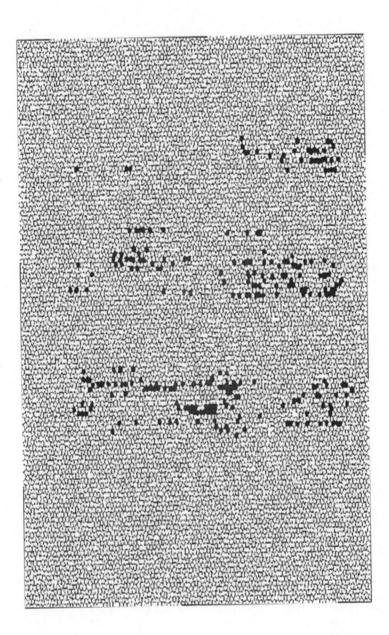

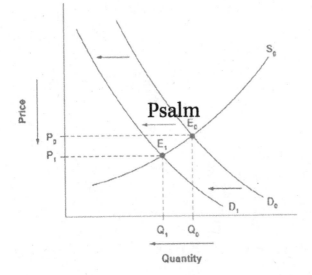

. . . the authentic *journey* will be restored to us, along with authentic life understood as a journey containing its whole meaning within itself.

—Guy Debord

His Eye on the Sparrow

—after Hanif

I guess black people can write about flowers at a time like this since every poem turns on itself. Starts one way to end another. We see it in nature too. How seed turns to leaf regardless of its earth, or the thought inside my head blossoms into a hyacinth with as sweet a scent. Even in dreams, thought's closest cousin, I often see Mamie Till. She walks the church aisle toward her son's body while wisteria bloats the casket's brim and papered bougainvillea bracts emerge from where his eye once was. An entire garden from the nutrients of once human. And not to mention all those awed birds that circle Emmett's pillowed corpse. So many in the tabernacle. Not predators of the fleshly bloom or harbingers of his God's descent, not refugees fleeing his exilic body but eternity's messengers. We, who pull breath, confuse death's irony. Whoever dies and is remembered stays living.

Animalia Repeating: A Pavlovian Account in Parts

I.   . . . organisms only learn when events violate their expectations.

—Robert A. Rescorla and Allan R. Wagner,

"A Theory of Pavlovian Conditioning"

News of the George Zimmerman verdict broke. My mother murmured, "Bad history repeats." My oldest son sank into his hands. My youngest numbed to a video game. My middle son rose from the sofa, adjusted his Little League T-shirt, and went to the bathroom.

After fifteen minutes I knocked on the door, found him crying on the floor. Under the sink, I held his head under my chin, his hand in mine. His forehead damp with stray tears. His slender body gradually calmed, he wondered, "Why do *they* hate me?" I suggested there was no *they*. Only fear and spit and tuning forks and hungry dogs and playful rats and people who are trying against all they've been taught to live with other people who are trying against all they've been taught to live. . . . Lulled by our racing thoughts, we fell asleep on cold tile.

II.   . . . conditioning depends upon the associative strength of all stimuli occur-
            ring on a trial . . .

—Rescorla and Wagner

Walking to a newly built shopping center, I overheard my sons: "We have to be careful. Make sure you take off your hat before we go inside the store. Pull up your pants. Don't put your hands in your pockets. Hold your arms where people can see them. Look people in the eye. Smile. Smile wider." I wanted to refute their instructions but stopped myself mid-gesture to utter, "Please come home before dinner."

III.   Somehow the organism appears to evaluate the probability with which
            shocks occur. . . .

—Rescorla and Wagner

Genuflecting at Mass, I stole fleeting glances of my sons' hands in prayer—tender, unburdened by veins or violence, unscathed. I prayed that whoever feared them would unlearn myth and snare. Hopeful, as every lukewarm

Catholic tends, until the priest's strange homily reminded me of Divinity's less-than-stellar record: "God's own son suffered and died."

Two sisters in the checkout line at a suburban Target stood in front of my son discussing their brother's recent misfortune. After a late-night tire blowout, their brother was assaulted and robbed while waiting for a tow. One sister remarked, "I miss Dad's Detroit." Careful to excuse himself, my son reached to grab the conveyor belt divider. The sister closest to him startled and pulled her wallet to her chest.

"Move up here . . ." one sister comforted another. "Near me . . . away."

"Affliction makes God appear to be absent for a time, more absent than a dead man, more absent than light in a completely dark cell . . ." were the repeating words of Simone Weil as I drove home. "During this absence there is nothing to love . . . ," skipped along the blemished curvature of memory's vinyl. Nearly convinced until my children laughed. Their laughter held presence sweetly behind me as if to insist *This here is love.*

We woke up stiff and uncomfortable from the bathroom floor in the middle of that July night. My son's eyelids red and swollen, he mumbled something akin to "Thanks, Mom." Washed his face and felt his way down the unlit hall toward his bed.

He slowed to pivot: "Mom, do you think what happened to Trayvon could happen again?" I searched for a way to disrupt how the human animal operates, briefly considered dogs and tuning forks, mice and levers, babies and white rats. I gently delivered what I believed to be truth.

Another summer and another heat-hollowed flesh. This time his name is Michael. My sons are in New Jersey with family. I am in Michigan. My phone rings.

"Mom, I read that Pavlov thing you gave me last year. How do you think the dogs felt?"

"Like Skinner's rats and pigeons—hungry, confused, terrified, controlled, alive. But, every single time, they still *felt.*"

Stichomythia

Why are you singing?

How do you know I am singing?

Because my ear tells me.

What if your ears lie?

Ears can't.

Why not?

Golden rule of aurality.

What does that mean?

Ears can't do what was done to them.

Revelations 1:14-16
from the *Book of the After Life Circus*
(Illustrated Parenthetical Edition)

[14] After Death and Hades were thrown into the lake and those with forgotten names doubly died, Saint Peter (pronounced Petra) stands outside the gate, waiting for Whosoever Will (the gate was a traffic warden kiosk with a warning: Don't Speed It Kills). For the deserving few, she stores 24 kt. gold in recycled gas containers—a welcome gift, if you will, for Whosoever. Closer to her hip, she holds the *Book of the After Life Circus* (a thin day planner with rushed notes she jots down as God hurries from one meeting to the next). [15] *Melt these canisters and make your streets,* she tells every new Whosoever Will (a loose translation since Saint Petra speaks Igbo). Of course, they never do. Whosoever Will rather hoped God might have taken care of paving their gold streets in anticipation of their arrival. Many of the Wills think Heaven should look more like Milton's Empyrean Divine (Milton was blind). And some demand immediate reincarnation upon realizing Saint Petra is a Nigerian woman (with very little patience for nonsense and delay), who coordinates her headwraps with hand-loomed cloth and prefers a burner phone to commercial anything (everything is bare essentials in Heaven and no one wears halos owing to carbon concerns). Further staggered to learn that Heaven is in Ibadan (not in the sky but certainly on any detailed map). [16] And since the mansions are Hussey Plaza hotel rooms, there's no provincial space for each soul (Saint Petra finds that belief laughable). *Silly,* she says, *you learn to live together in Heaven, one on top of another, until your spirits transmute into something (somewhat) deserving of Paradise.*

December

—after "Harp" by Eileen Myles

Once

when I

was in

space

spiraling

toward

galactic

oblivion

I set up a Christmas
tree in the season
of greeting and return.
Right there in the family
room. I covered that year's
arboreal sacrifice in multi-
ethnic lights as reminder
that dark relief comes
in every hue.

Carolers sang outside
my window, hymns I
didn't know I'd
memorized until
I found myself
mouthing the lyrics

with precision: *O*
Come, All
Ye Faithful . . . O
Holy Night.
Inside, children
passed pleasures
on heirloom dishes
as I excavated
a moldy box
in search of
the white angel
holding a star
that with my brown
sharpie I suffused
into a black angel
holding a star.

I ascended a stepstool to
crown that daft Fraser
while praying a celestial
petition I knew, if granted,
would level me:
bring them back,
plastic nebulae
of niggardly
light, return
who's loved
me worst.

Haunting Axioms

Some ghosts don't know they're dead.
This is also true of the living.

Some ghosts feel trapped on earth.
This is also true of the living.

Some ghosts re-enact their past.
This is also true of the living.

Some ghosts regret what's behind.
This is also true for some living.

Some ghosts have not earned rest.
This is also true for some living.

Some ghosts never seem to forget.
This is not quite true for the living.

Some ghosts return to their wound.
This is always true of the living.

Goodnight, Gibbous Moon: A Wake-up Story

In the great bleak room
there was a telephone
and a big buffoon
and a picture of a sheep
shooting up the moon
and there were three
heels of bread
asleep on the bed
and a half-plunged needle
and a flour-coated weevil
and past due tolls
and attic holes
and a storm and a funnel
and a windblown tunnel
and a bat and a shove
and the question of love
and a comb of kinked hair
and a frayed wicker chair
and the slowed steady crush
of all the elders insisting I *hushhhh*

Goodnight, Fog Room.
Goodnight, Gibbous Moon.
Goodnight, Heels of Bread.
Goodnight, Family Bed.
Goodnight, Needle.
Goodnight, Weevil.
Goodnight, Late Toll.
Goodnight, Roof Hole.
Goodnight, Storm Funnel.
Goodnight, Wind Tunnel.
Goodnight, Fierce Shove.
Goodnight, unLove.

Goodnight, Kinked Hair.
Goodnight, Wicker Chair.
Goodnight, Steadied Crush
And goodnight to the elders all whispering *hushhhh*.
Goodnight, Bat Savior.
Goodnight, Truth or Dare.
Goodnight chaos everywhere.

Ars Poetica, 2021

I lived
a question.

Survived
the answer.

Subtext for Troubled Times

I imagine, by now, you're no longer wondering,

though I never answered your question:

What do you think the author intended?

One of those rhetorical numbers; the breath

provided response. Surely you're somewhere

deep in thought. Finger to mouth or thumbing

some mug's brim while thousands of fingerprint

parabola hold me in the grooves long after

you'd glided your index across my raised

mast's braille. Scissoring, your good hand

high, the other dropped down, I agreed

with you—100 words per minute.

But, then, I stopped count at 10.

So little language is lost

in heightened dimension,

in the small space of asking:

Will you read this poem, my love?

Then crisply opening my body

across your lap.

Nevertheless

Praise to the father holding his sleeping daughter on the 52nd Street trolley
    To the daughter dreaming through the pothole thrum

Praise to the diabetic with shorn feet & sugarcane blood
    To the anxious nerve through left hip & lower spine
    To those flying axons on their routes

Praise to the red-headed Rasta & his ganja-laced T-shirt
    To the Vietnam vet at Cass Corridor holding a sign
    To the sign which reads: "Not homeless just strugglin'"

Praise to the barbers calming the fatherless in their chairs
    To the mothers trying not to overhear this soothing
    To soothing

Praise to razed skylines & ruins
    To whatever replaces the horizon
    To the lost toddler who refused to speak to strangers
    To the strangers who would not let him be lost

Praise to sisters in love with whoever won't love them
    To others in love with whoever won't bother

Praise to the lovers who left lessons,
        those lovers who left scars
    To the memory of topography,
        raised surface, smooth to touch
    To id's frail shards & ego's fringed edge

Praise to boys who make beeswax fingernails
    To little girls who wear fatigues & eye black
Praise to those often overlooked,
        the chronic overlooking

Praise to Miss Toto, Bambi Banks, Pearl Harbour
    To bombs that never landed
    To satellites that couldn't be coaxed to Earth
    To bodily grail that won't hold a lie

Praise to beauty that doesn't suffer rules
    To dollar store chic & sleek vintage tins
    To loose wave & tight curl
    To wanting to be & being

Praise to love's revival
    To incising shame's jugular
    To the unrecalled, misjudged
        & half-remembered

Praise to the hard-won win against Chronos
    To the stone wrapped in swaddling,
        the eaglet's nesting latibule,
        barren sirens rearing urchin,
        the eye uncrossed, uncrowed

Praise to scuffed boot houses
        children running over frayed laces

Praise to the old kitchen, half-gutted,
      its April gnats & snowbank flies,
      its mice hugging sweet corners

Praise to that which endures
    To old doors, layers of paint,
        years of storm beating solid oak
    To the gable roof that is a ceiling,
        the coffered ceiling that is also a floor

Praise to what shoulders weight
    To brackets & load-bearing walls
        beams & spindly skeletons
        sacred geometry & tangents
    To levees & pregnant summers
        the buckshot-ridden body
        wheeling to coilspring

Praise to the ground unfastening
    To the thorny or fertile soil
    To each seraph's flutterwind
        & every earthworm's bristle
        entwined in waltz of welcome

Praise to the body relenting to dust,
        the spirit yielding ascent

Praise to all who rejoice in becoming
Amen to all who transform in return

On Equilibrium

cul-

tivated and improved.

Upon equal, or nearly equal

profits, most men will chuse to employ

their capitals rather in the improvement and

cultivation of land than either in manufactures

or in foreign trade. The man who employs his capital in land has

it more under his view and

command, and his **fortune is much less liable to** accidents than that of the trader,

who is

obliged frequently to commit it, not only to the **wind**s **and** the **wave**s, but to the more

uncertain elements of human folly and injustice, by giving great credits in distant countries

to **[those] with** whose **character** and situation he can seldom be thoroughly acquainted. The

capital

of the landlord, on the contrary, which is fixed in the improvement of his land, seems to be

as well secured as the nature of human affairs can **[allow]** The **beauty** of the country

besides,

the pleasures of **a** country life, the tranquility of min**d**, which it **promise**s, and

wherever

the injustice of human laws does not disturb it, the independency which it

really affords, have

charms that more or less attract every body; and as **to cultivate the**

ground was the original

destination of man, so **in every stage of** his **existence** he seems

to retain a predilection for

this primitive employment.

Eviction

—for Wisława

As if I created this
pyramid of obey and exist.
Between the breathturn stares
of others, also exiled, and those
who called me all but my name,
I nearly forgot that I could,
unlike Lot's wife, glance back
for the answers—some threads
of truth where memory faltered.
In sooth, that snake was not a reptile.
The fruit of good and evil
was a flower of wasps, not an apple.
I was less inbred rib—more accurately,
unbred. Love was often anguished and
paradise looked like anybody's
milkweed garden. I didn't
beg Adam's pardon and never
asked *why me, O Lord?* No
proverbs would suffice when
genesis is what is and was what
was. I looked, instead, to the present
as the past cracked underfoot,
lowered into riverbeds. The waters
rose below and leagues above flaming
vines enveloped the stairs to heaven
glister by glister. Due east, fly ash
blanketed each morning glory
I named in light, pocked
the night phlox perfumed distant
moons ago. I vowed from the eye
of that reckoning, fates among
Eves would not be the same:

If one sister is silenced into salt
without body that remembers,
then I will batter my cymbals
bearing witness for us both
with what body still remains.

Acknowledgments

All thanks to the editors of the following publications, in which these poems—often in earlier versions—appeared:

Academy of American Poets, Poem-a-Day (May 17, 2019, guest editor Victoria Chang): "etymology," https://poets.org/poem/etymology

Georgia Review (Winter 2022): "Eviction," "The Troubles," "Severance," and "elegy for the moaner, 2016"

Gulf Coast (Summer/Fall 2021): "9am: Working Class Bedtime Story"

Indiana Review: "Positive Curvature," "Camelot"

Last Call: Poems on Alcoholism, Addiction, & Deliverance, eds. Sarah Gorham and Jeffrey Skinner (Louisville, KY: Sarabande Books, 1997): "Legacy Costs"

Los Angeles Review of Books: "The Rules of Attention"

Michigan Quarterly Review: *Michigan Quarterly Review* (blog): "The Cost of the Floss," "Meeting Wittgenstein at the Circus" (as "Meeting Wittgenstein at the Playscape"), and "Animalia Repeating: A Pavlovian Account in Parts"; "Nevertheless: An Ecstatic Ode" (as "Black Ecstatic Ode") 58, no. 3 (Summer 2019)

Missouri Review (September 23, 2013): "Swindle"

Mosaic: "Subtext for Troubled Times"

On the Seawall (January 7, 2019): "Revelations from the Book of the After Life Circus" [as "Illustrated Revelations 20:14–16 (from the Parenthetical Version)]

South Carolina Review (Fall 2022): as Dee Matthews, "to tell you three things on my mind is to tell you about quarantine and temperance"

Vinyl: "-Icity"

Virginia Quarterly Review (Summer 2021): "Ars Poetica, 1979"

The Volta (November 2015): "The Revolt of Gryllacridadae" (as "Gryllacridadae, The Impoverished")

Women's Studies Quarterly (Spring/Summer 2014): "March, 1969"

Zocalo Public Square (August 14, 2020): "Adam Smith on Division" (as "Inherited Divide")

A special thanks to the institutions that have offered fellowships and space to think through this work—Bryn Mawr College, University of Edinburgh, Bodleian Libraries, the Pew Foundation, the City of Philadelphia, the Academy of American Poets, James Merrill House, and the University of Michigan Helen Zell Writers' Program.

I owe a debt to my friends and colleagues—some beloveds read earlier versions of these poems and helped me to figure out my thoughts, like Arisa White and Nora Chassler, and others gave comfort through their kindness or inspiration through their brilliance, including the Detroit School, Dr. Sonya Lott, Carl Phillips, Vievee Francis, Matthew Olzmann, Gregory Pardlo, A. Van Jordan, Chris Abani, Naomi Jackson, Cynthia Dewi Oka, Sham-e Ali, Dr. Jonah Mixon Webster, Phillip B. Williams, Erin Belieu, Ernesto Mercer, Dan Torday, Michelle London, Syd Zolf, Khadijah Queen, Linda Gregerson, Haya Alfarhan, Noor Ibn Najam, Amy Beth Sisson, Aricka Foreman, Nandi Comer, Tommye Blount, Gala Mukomolova, Yolanda Wisher, Sanam Sherrif, Laynie Browne, Gillian Eaton, Rachel McKibbens, Mecca Jamillah Sullivan, Danez Smith, Keith Wilson, Hanif Abdurraqib, Douglas Kearney, francine j. harris, Ladan Osman, and every single student I've ever had the pleasure to teach or challenge.

I remain ever grateful for Rob McQuilkin, Kathy Belden, Don Patterson, and Colette Bryce—four beautiful and luminous souls who believed in this work early on.

Special thanks to my dearly departed ancestors who watch and act on behalf of my highest good.

And, of course, I am grateful for my family! To Rae and Mommy for their strength. To Lisa for her wisdom. To Emery for his impassioned love, holding, zeal, patience, belief, and mind. To Trey for his resilience and determination. To Wes for his vision and faith (and the title). To Eli for his humor and logic. To Willow for her magic and sight. We made it through to the other side . . . together. #TMFAW.

And to anyone I haven't named, please charge it to my head and not my heart.

Notes and Sources

Select texts from this book place the author, economist Adam Smith, and social theorist Guy Debord in conversation through their work. Adam Smith (1723–1790) was a Scottish economist and moral philosopher and is often known as "the Father of Capitalism." One of his best-known works, *An Inquiry into the Nature and Causes of the Wealth of Nations* (1776), became the foundational text of modern economics, capitalism, and the free market. Smith forwarded the invisible hand theory in which self-interest was at the heart of a thriving economy—people would help one another economically because it was in their best interest. The belief in self-interest is the basis of modern free-market capitalism. The edition I used was *An Inquiry into the Nature and Causes of the Wealth of Nations*, Glasgow Edition of the Works of Adam Smith, 2 vols., eds. R. H. Campbell and A. S. Skinner (first published 1776; repr., Oxford: Oxford University Press, 1976; repr., ebook, Indianapolis, IN: Liberty Fund, 1981).

Conversely, Guy Debord (1931–1994) was one of the founding members for the Situationist International (1957–1972), an organization composed of interdisciplinary libertarian Marxists, who posited that in late-stage capitalism social relations of all kinds would deteriorate and be mediated through objects—products that one can buy, sell, or fetishize. He authored *The Society of the Spectacle* (*La Société du spectacle*) in 1967, a book of 221 aphoristic theses and the foundational text of the Situationist International movement. Debord's work exposed the ways in which capitalist self-interest lends itself to the spectacle as human beings are reduced to what they possess, and possession is reduced to mere appearance. In this advanced system of capitalism, the author argues, the body itself becomes a fetishized commodity.

The title of this book is derived from the phrase "bread and circus," which first appeared in the poet Juvenal's "Satura X." Written in AD 100, the original, according to the Latin Library (http://www.perseus.tufts.edu/hopper/text ?doc=Perseus:text:2007.01.0093:book=4:poem=10&highlight=satura) reads: "*iam pridem, ex quo suffragia nulli / vendimus, effudit curas; nam qui dabat olim / imperium fasce legiones omnia, nunc se / continet atque duas tantum res anxius optat, / panem et circenses.*" When translated, the verse reads: "Long ago they have thrown overboard all anxiety. For that sovereign people that once gave away military command, consulships, legions, and every thing, now bridles its desires, and limits its anxious longings to two things only—bread, and the games of the circus!" The metonymic phrase implies that people in power appease through distraction.

The four through-composed section titles of the book pay homage to John Coltrane's *A Love Supreme*, released in 1965. Musicologist Dr. John Edwartowski calls the through-composition "a rhetorically continuous series that includes exposition, development, and recapitulation."

Sources

Epigraph, p. vii: From *The Satires of Juvenal, Persius, Sulpicia, and Lucilius*, trans. Rev. Lewis Evans (London: Henry G. Bohn, 1850).

"Acknowledgment"

Epigraph: Adam Smith, "Of the Principle Which Gives Occasion to the Division of Labour," book I, chap. II in *The Wealth of Nations*, pp. 26–27. Graphic image: Wikimedia Commons contributors, "Production-Possibility Frontier," Fig. 1, https://en.wikipedia.org/wiki/Production%E2%80%93possibility_frontier.

"Debord's Redacted Spectacle": Palimpsestic extraction from Guy Debord, section 69 of "Unity and Division Within Appearances," in *The Society of the Spectacle*, trans. and annotated Ken Knabb (Berkeley, CA: Bureau of Public Secrets, 2014). Photo of the author's mother and father from personal archive.

"The Troubles": Poem refers to the Bogside Massacre (Bloody Sunday) that occurred on January 30, 1972, in Derry, Northern Ireland. During the conflict, British soldiers killed twenty-six civilians.

"Smith on Exchange": Extraction from Adam Smith, "Of the Principle Which Gives Occasion to the Division of Labor," book I, chap. II in *The Wealth of Nations*, p. 26.

"On Origin and Use": Extraction from Adam Smith, "Of the Origin and Use of Money," book I, chap. IV, in *The Wealth of Nations*, pp. 37–39.

"On Supper": Extraction from Adam Smith, "Of the Principle Which Gives Occasion to the Division of Labor," book I, chap. II in *The Wealth of Nations*, pp. 26–27.

"Papa Teaches the Hard Six at a Gulf Station, 1980": In the aftermath of the 1979 oil shock, oil prices continued to rise and triggered economic recession, intensifying the allure of the underground economy. The hard six is a term used in craps to signify a high risk/high reward gamble. A hard six is achieved by rolling threes on a pair of six-sided dice. There is a 3 percent probability of rolling a hard six, compared to a 14 percent probability of rolling six by other combinations.

"Resolution"

Epigraph: Adam Smith, "Of the Accumulation of Capital, or of Productive and Unproductive Labour," book II, chap. III in *The Wealth of Nations*, pp. 341–42. Graphic image: Wikimedia Commons contributors, "Production-Possibility Frontier," Fig. 5, https://en.wikipedia.org/wiki/Production%E2%80%93possibility_frontier.

"On Division": Extraction and extension from Adam Smith, "On the Principle Which Gives Occasion to the Division of Labour," book I, chap. II in *The Wealth of Nations*, pp. 25–26.

"On Real Costs": Extraction from Adam Smith, "Of the Real and Nominal Price of Commodities, or Their Price in Labour, and Their Price in Money," book I, chap. V in *The Wealth of Nations*, pp. 47–48.

"The Revolt of Gryllacridadae": Inspired by the Radiolab episode "Killer Empathy" (February 6, 2012) in which Dr. Jeff Lockwood explains the instincts of family Gryllacridadae. Available at: https://radiolab.org/episodes/185551-killer-empathy.

"On Debt": Extraction and extension from Adam Smith, "Of Public Debts," book V, chap. III in *The Wealth of Nations*, pp. 909–10.

"Pursuance"

Epigraph: Guy Debord, section 66 of "Unity and Division Within Appearances" in *The Society of the Spectacle*, trans. and annotated Ken Knabb (Berkeley, CA: Bureau of Public Secrets, 2014), p. 27. Graphic image: Wikimedia Commons contributors, "File:Positive Externality.png," https://commons.wikimedia.org/w/index.php?title=File:Positive_Externality.png&oldid=654107006).

"We Was Kings": Photo taken inside the walls of Edinburgh Castle from author's personal archive. Though the historic record is largely silent, there is archaeological evidence of sub-Saharan and Northern African migration to Britain during the Roman Empire, which could explain the presence of the darker hair and strong African features of the Scots kings in the mural.

"On Mobility": Extraction from Adam Smith, "Of the Division of Stock," book II, chap. I in *The Wealth of Nations*, pp. 281–82.

"American Ouroboros": The contrapuntal mentions the word "pornotrope," which is borrowed from the scholarship of Hortense Spillers and examined in the sixth chapter, "Depravation: Pornotropes," of Alexander G. Weheliye's *Habeas Viscus: Racializing Assemblages, Biopolitics, and Black Feminist Theories of the Human* (Durham, NC: Duke University Press, 2014), p. 90.

"-Icity": On December 30, 2012, in a double tragedy, an eight-year-old Detroit girl was stabbed to death in her home by her drug-addicted mother. All names have been redacted. Gina Damron and Elisha Anderson, "Little Girl Lost," *Detroit Free Press*, January 24, 2013, pp. 1–6a.

"Logical Disjunction": In classical logic, logical disjunction states that one or both connecting statements are true. Graphic image: Wikimedia Commons contributors, "File: Multigrade operator all xor nothing," https://commons.wikimedia.org/wiki/File: Multigrade_operator_all_xor_nothing.svg.

"The Broke Diet": David Blair, "Enough Rope," MP3 audio, track 6 on Bandcamp The Line (2009), https://blairdetroit.bandcamp.com/releases.

"Debord's Deconstructed Spectacle, Before": Extraction and extension from Guy Debord, sections 1–7 of "Separation Perfected" in *The Society of the Spectacle*, trans. and annotated Ken Knabb (Berkeley, CA: Bureau of Public Secrets, 2014), p. 2.

"O Pleas": Extraction from Adam Smith, "Of the Accumulation of Capital, or of Productive and Unproductive Labour," book II, chap. III in *The Wealth of Nations,* " pp. 330–31.

"Debord's Deconstructed Spectacle, After": A Voronoi diagram of the poem "Debord's Deconstructed Spectacle, Before." The Voronoi diagram is used in different computational fields to encode or determine proximity for a given set of objects, or sites. Cells define the set of points and the proximity of those points to one another.

"Psalm"

Epigraph: Guy Debord, section 178 of "Environmental Planning" in *The Society of the Spectacle*, trans. Donald Nicholson-Smith (New York: Zone Books, 1995), p. 126. Graphic image: Wikimedia Commons contributors, "File: Higher Compensation for Postal Workers - A Four-Step Analysis.jpg," (b) Shift in demand, https://commons.wikimedia.org/w/index.php?title=File:Higher_Compensation_for_Postal_Workers-A_Four-Step_Analysis.jpg&oldid=472231420.

"Animalia Repeating: A Pavlovian Account in Parts" epigraphs to prose blocks: Section I: Robert A. Rescorla and Allan R. Wagner, "A Theory of Pavlovian Conditioning: Variations in the Effectiveness of Reinforcement and Nonreinforcement," in *Classical Conditioning II: Current Research and Theory,* eds. Abraham H. Black and William F. Prokasy (New York: Appleton-Century-Crofts, 1972), p. 75; Section II: ibid., p. 74; Section III: ibid., p. 87; Section IV: John B. Watson and Rosalie Rayner, "Conditioned Emotional Reactions," *Journal of Experimental Psychology* 3, no. 1 (February 1920), p. 3; Section V: Rescorla and Wagner, p. 94; the Simone Weil quote is from "The Love of God and Affliction," in *Waiting for God*, trans. Emma Craufurd (New York: G. P. Putnam & Sons, 1951), pp. 120–21; Section VI: B. F. Skinner "A Brief Survey of Operant Behavior" (1938), B. F. Skinner Foundation, https://www.bfskinner.org/wp-content/uploads/2014/02/A_brief_survey_of_operant_behavior.pdf; Section VII: B. F. Skinner, *The Behavior of Organisms: An Experimental Analysis* (New York: Appleton-Century-Crofts, 1938), p. 462.

"Revelations 1:14–16 from the *Book of the After Life Circus* (Illustrated Parenthetical Edition)": Photo used with permission from the Chris Abani photographic archive.

"Nevertheless": Photos used with permission from the Chris Abani photographic archive.

"On Equilibrium": Extraction and extension Adam Smith, "Of the Natural Progress of Opulence," book III, chap. I in *The Wealth of Nations*, pp. 387–88.

"Eviction": "Breathturn" is from Pierre Joris's 1995 English translation of the German kenning *Atemwende*, which is also the title of Paul Celan's 1967 collection of poems.

About the Author

Airea D. Matthews was Philadelphia's poet laureate from 2022 to 2023. Her first collection of poems was the critically acclaimed *Simulacra*, which won the 2016 Yale Series of Younger Poets award. Her work has appeared in *The New York Times*, *Gulf Coast*, *VQR*, *Best American Poets*, *American Poet*, *Literary Hub*, *Harvard Review*, and elsewhere. Matthews holds a BA in economics from the University of Pennsylvania as well as an MFA from the Helen Zell Writers' Program and an MPA from the Gerald R. Ford School of Public Policy, both at the University of Michigan. A Pew Fellow, she is an associate professor and codirects the poetry program at Bryn Mawr College.